OSTRICH CREEK

TOM AND OTHER SURVIVORS

by

GILLIAN BENCE-JONES

Published by
New Hope International
20 Werneth Avenue, Gee Cross,
Hyde, Cheshire, SK14 5NL, UK

1999

To Mark, remembering Petra

Acknowledgments are due to the editors of the following publications in which some of these poems have previously appeared: **The Daily Telegraph; Envoi; Fat Chance; Krax; New Hope International Writing** and **Rialto**

All poems © Gillian Bence-Jones, 1999
Introduction © Hugh Massingberd, 1999

Cover photograph: Tom Baker (see p.52)

For New Hope International omnibus subscribers this Special Edition Chapbook forms Volume 20 #4

British Library Cataloguing in Publication Data. A catalogue record for this book is available from the British Library.

ISBN 0 903610 22 1

Contents

Acknowledgements &c	2
Contents	3
Introduction by Hugh Massingberd	4
Butterflies	7
Safe As Houses	8
Spinster in the Sun	9
The Three Sisters	10
Philomel with Melody	12
Silver Wedding Bed	12
Blind Windows	13
Strangers & Pilgrims	14
Eleanor	15
Gulf	16
Last Laugh	18
Peacocks and Palanquins	19
Widely Rude	22
Malabar Surf	23
Round The World	24
Daily Walk	26
Mary's Robe	27
Hymn Modern	28
Cup Bearer	30
Garden by the Sea	32
Tree from the Tagus	33
Plastic Country	34
Remission	35
Sackville Cousins	36
Charm	37
Survivors	38
Twilight	39
Flight	40
Decoy Pond	41
The First	42
The Golden Ring	44
Wrong Animal	44
New Life	45

Quack	46
Sudden Death	46
Apparition	47
Far Flowers	47
Drishane	48
My Father	49
Horse Power	50
Spring Ending	51
Tom	52
Sea Beast	56
Sea of Faith	56
Publications from New Hope International	57

INTRODUCTION

GILLIAN Bence-Jones was the first poet I ever met. As a gauche and callow youth not long out of school — where the doctrinaire Leavisite "Eng Lit" teacher had succeeded in putting me right off "text-book poetry" — my ignorance of metre, rhythm, scansion, indeed everything to do with verse, was total. (Still is, come to think of it.) The only living poet — this was the end of the Sixties — that made any appeal was John Betjeman. Unlike the crashing and incomprehensible bores of the so-called "Beat Generation" then in fashion, Betjeman's expression of understated but deeply felt English emotions struck a chord. Above all, he had a strong sense of place. I wrote him a fan letter but, alas, never met the great man.

On meeting Gillian Bence-Jones, then living in a farmhouse overlooking the River Orwell on her parents' idyllic estate in Suffolk, I was immediately struck by her liberating lack of self-consciousness. Acutely self-conscious and inhibited myself, I was at first disconcerted by her tendency to sing snatches of songs (often hymns) or recite poetry on our walks together across countryside that seemed unchanged since Constable's day. But I soon learnt that for Gill poetry was one of life's pleasures to be enjoyed in the same way as, say, the search for a wild orchid in the marshes or a swim in the Orwell in October (during a freak Indian summer, I should explain). For her, it was natural to express her feelings and observations of her surroundings in verse.

On subsequent visits to the farmhouse at Nacton, I had the privilege of hearing her recite, face to face, some of the poems that were to form her first published collection, *Bacton: Where Two Rivers Rise*. My initial embarrassment at such intimate auditions gave way to a new enjoyment of what poetry could do — generalise the particular, unlock personal feelings, manage in a short space to be funny, sad and elegiac all at the same time. I could also actually understand what she was getting at — a refreshing change from other modern poets who take refuge in wilful obscurity. It was an education, one I had lacked from the Leavisite.

Like Betjeman, Bence-Jones is inspired by a sense of place. She celebrates the essential Englishness of country life and country people, rejoices in their inbuilt conservatism and modestly disguised sensitivity to nature and kindliness, listens sympathetically to their troubles, sings the praises of traditional Anglicanism while mocking the absurdities of trendy trimmers, neophiliac modernisers and the dreaded Eurocrats. Her voice is the voice of no-nonsense Suffolk: clear, lyrical and straight to the point. Not for nothing did that great English writer Eric Blair (albeit of Scots ancestry) choose the pen-name of "George Orwell".

Gill's father, the late Mr Pretyman of Orwell Park, was christened George back in 1895; and it was from him and her mother, the former Camilla Gurdon, that their only child acquired not only her love of poetry but its natural place in the scheme of things, along with history, flora, fauna, the country and its traditional pastimes. Both Gill's parents were from notably long-established Suffolk families. Indeed the Pretymans and Gurdons are among only half-a-dozen "Visitation" dynasties in the county (that is to say surviving families who held land at the time the Heralds made their Visitations to inspect coats of arms and pedigrees in the sixteenth and early seventeenth centuries). This powerful feeling of rootedness informs and illuminates Gillian Bence-Jones's poetry.

Her long pedigree gives her the confidence to tackle historical themes — as in the stirring Elizabethan nautical poem *Round the World* in this new collection - without affectation but with no shortage of romance either. Sometimes, too, one hears the melancholy echoes of the Somme. Like Siegfried Sassoon, Gillian Bence-Jones is at her best contrasting the horrors of the Western Front with the pastoral beauty of home. For her father, like so many of his generation, had been deeply affected by his experiences in the Great War and seldom spoke about it — though I was once privileged enough to hear him recall the bravery of a hitherto largely unknown great-uncle of mine. Gill would listen enthralled to her father's contemporary, Tom Baker, the redoubtable keeper of the duck decoy on the Orwell estate, who had total recall of everything he had ever seen, 'so to talk to him was to be on the Somme'.

Gill has captured this splendid character both in verse, and in a haunting prose-poem that she sent to me at *The Daily Telegraph*, where I was then working on the obituaries desk, when Tom died aged 96 in 1991. I felt proud and privileged to be able to publish it, and subsequently to include it in a collected volume of obituaries. Several people have told me that it is the best thing in the book. Apart from the dramatic and fascinating material about the First World War (except in one particular: he would never tell how he won his Military Medal), it is full of charm and wry humour; 'At 94 he was still digging and scything, and always took a walk every day, his notion of a walk was seldom less than a mile and often about five. Tom Baker was a good Christian but preferred not to talk about it.'

My favourite bit is when Gill tells of the time Sir Peter Scott took over the decoy. The celebrity held out his hand, with what he hoped was a modest smile, and said: 'Is this the man who knows more about duck than I do?' Tom's reply ensured that the rapport between the two men was never quite what it might have been. 'I reckon I do,' he said.

There is the direct voice of Suffolk all right, and nobody is better attuned to it than Gillian Bence-Jones. But it would be quite wrong to suggest that her poetry is exclusively concerned with her native heath. She has the true poet's instinct of registering impressions wherever she finds herself — whether in Ireland, where her husband, the author Mark Bence-Jones's family comes from, or on her travels with him in India and the Middle East. Similarly her ear is as acute to the contemporary experiences of her teenaged younger daughter in the late 1990s as it is to the nuances of her parents' generation from the beginning of the 20th century. The backchat of the Belvoir in the Fifties is as much grist to her poetic mill as the idiocies of millennial jargon. Gillian Bence-Jones is not predictable: she is an original, individual and stimulating poet for all seasons.

Hugh Massingberd

BUTTERFLIES

On the aubretia
Again, two tortoiseshells
And all summer to come.

SAFE AS HOUSES

The pillared hall
Harbours stairs;
A cluttered table;
A picture of my Mother
Riding.

Under the umber steps
And treble clef there's
A cupboard full of junk.
I must have spent a month
In there.

When the searchlights crossed
Looking like swords
And the watchdog guns
Barked on the coast
We went in there.

My father read aloud
The riverbank,
The wild wood,
Punctuated
By thumps.

We were snug as mole
In badger's den.
I remember asking
If it was wrong to pray
For an air raid.

SPINSTER IN THE SUN

I had a cousin
Called Lavender.
Crossed in love
And not allowed
To work; she turned
To chocolate and went
To Kenya.

Rose creams in the
Kikuyu country.
Caramel in Eldoret;
Till she resembled
A river horse.
People found her funnier
Than ever.

When she was young her mother,
The central heating
Of the household, was killed
In a car smash.
Her mother, hoping
For loveliness, called her
Lavender.

THE THREE SISTERS

When the wind blows
On the moor
They wander here
That went before.
The wine of heather
And the bread of stones
Are spread for them
And they return
As we assume
Their truthful eyes.

Emily adored
The hump-backed bridge
Whose string
Shoots quivering arrows
At the rocks above.

Anne loved
The hollow
Where green plates
Of primroses
Filled up with cream.

Branwell took the path
To the pub and Charlotte
Was left alone.

Her father hardly counted
For he had his study.
Yet he played Laban
And Jacob served
Fourteen years and the time
Seemed short for the love
He bore her.
If her father had given in
Sooner; or later, perhaps...

But the sweep of the hills
Is so and no other way.
There have been enough
Miracles here.
Scorned spinsters;
Poor clergymen;
Provincial people
Blazed
And the fire
Still warms our hands.
Among so much
Buried, burned,
Forgotten;
A number of worlds
Survived.

PHILOMEL WITH MELODY

To discover a unicorn, radiant
In a cowslip ride;
Leaf shadow dappled
While nightingales sang;
Must've been startling
As lightning. O but too beautiful
To be real. Did you
Call to it or admire
From not too near?
Or were you a virgin,
Wait till it bowed
Its samite head
Into your lap.
So I felt
When I found
I was next
To the Poet Laureate
At dinner.

SILVER WEDDING BED

Waking warm
I feel your flesh
All along
And the world
Is warmed for me
By your desire.

BLIND WINDOWS

Ardfry above the vigil water
So loved
And left to rot.

Bang! Bang! Marriage and class
Fly apart like overcooked chestnuts.
The water from Ardfry, lovely as ever,
But don't go down, there's poison in the pot.
The beeches burn in autumn
And soon may burn in sober fact.
Trees and gentry live together
And fall apart.

The servants' footsteps died away
Down to the basement. The children shout
In other places. The house waits
For someone who may never come.

Toll the bell and call the roll
Of ardent Irish houses
Moldering to cold harbours.
Coole, Convamore, Castle Freke, Donard, Desart
Does it matter? Not to the blind.
Does beauty matter?

STRANGERS & PILGRIMS

Born beautiful
We drift through being ugly bores
To being bones.

Leave everything
And slide into the void.
The body shrinks
From annihilation.
The mind shrinks
From no longer being
It's thinking self.

The marigolds
In the flood meadows
Soon fade.
The loved dog
Has to be put down.

Friends, family go
And are no more seen.
Intolerable sorrow;
No end to the ending
And the grief.

But we have hope
Of 'a better country.'
Where we don't know
And most likely
Couldn't understand
If we did know.
Andrewes said of Golgotha
'The place of bones
Has become a place of angels.'

ELEANOR

Born when the weather turned
In whitethorn time she brought us gifts
The west wind stroked the opened trees
And swung the tassels of wisteria,
Laburnum, lilac. After two dust months
The soft rain laughed in the pipes;
The grass smelt of growth
And in the blue and blossom wood
The nightingale was jubilant
To bring her welcome home.

GULF

Aquaba
Just over
The cobalt water:
Set in the porphyry country
We explored
When honey came
With carelessness
In that white town
And jagged wilderness.
Away, away
Further falls
The Wadi Rhum,
The mighty rift
Between now
When we are old
And then
When we, young,
Slept in Petra:
Red pillars
Turned to purple
As the sun went down.
No cave
In Eilat
But room number
Five hundred and eighty four:
No curves
But egg box compartments.

Yesterday we tried
A glass-bottomed boat
Which dimmed
The dazzling fish.
The Israeli commentary
Quacked of Aquaba:
'Population at present
Much greater than that of Eilat.'
Aquaba
Just over
The crystal water;
Another country
Where we, walking
Between the cliffs,
Stepped out
Into the heart
Of a rose.

LAST LAUGH

'On the Somme in sixteen
I was in the Orficer's mess
And you'll hardly credit it
But they was a' talking about longevity,
Solemn as judges.
The Adjutant he hold,

"You don't need nawthin' but clean air;
Draw it deep into your lungs
Every day." Along come a shell:
The dug-out fill up with smoke
And dust. We was all a'cawghin'.
"Yes," say the Colonel
"I see what you mean."'
And the ninety-five year old
Laughed so hard he threw
Himself back in his chair.

PEACOCKS AND PALANQUINS

Fanny Eden,
All ringlets and crinoline,
Went to the jungle
In a palanquin.
A Rajah,
In gold kincob,
With his khitmagars
Holding torches,
Gave her a spotted deer
Two peacocks
And some honey.
She wrote to a friend
Eleanor Grosvenor: 'My little deer
Is such a treasure
He travels in my howdah
And I hope hides his face
When they shoot any
Of his connections.
He trots after me
From one tent to another
In the most majestic manner.
This morning the jungle
Was burning; we had to make
A detour to get by,
The bearers singing
As a melancholy chorus
"Jeldu, jeldu, kubadar!"
William and I
Strolled about

On an elephant
This afternoon.
Wild roses and reed grass
On tumbled ground
Higher than one's head
And always the far away hills.
We found an enormous
Skeleton of a snake -
Ariffe said a boa constrictor
And that it was thirty foot long.
I trust none of its relations
Are about because
We shall hardly have room
For them in our tent.
The camp is always followed
By a quantity of pariah dogs,
Half-wild creatures
Who belong to nobody.
One has followed us
All the way from Barrackpore.
Rather a handsome one but perhaps
Slightly related to the jackal tribe.
As he attached himself
Particularly to William
It has required the united attentions
Of the two hundred and sixty people
Who comprise the camp
To keep him and my deer separate.
The instant the dog
Looked that way everybody
Began shrieking.

This evening both animals
Were missing and I found them
Together. The deer always
Walks straight up to any animal
It sees, the impertinence
Of the proceeding was too much
For the spirit of the pariah dog
And they have been licking
Each other's faces.'
Later, hotter: when perhaps
The dream had darkened
For her brother George,
The Governor-General.
Thunder clouds coming up
From Afghanistan,
And her nephew William
The Military-Secretary:
George was bored.
William had a fit
Of 'the Bariellies'.
But Fanny, older, frailer,
Still allowed the haunting
Ridiculous tune to sing to her.
She wrote 'They took us to
Lord Cornwallis' tomb that looks
Quite fresh from the sculptor.
We saw the Church lighted up
As we came near and gave
Another shock to Mr Macnaghten's
Constitution by going in without
A single aide-de-camp.

We mean to reform
And behave better,
Though as it is,
It seems to me
We are always
Sailing about
In a cloud
Of peacock's feathers
Silver sticks
And golden umbrellas.'

WIDELY RUDE

Wodehouse, PG,
Is very rude
About poetry.
All the same
There is no doubt
He knows a lot
To be rude about.

MALABAR SURF

Always more waves
Wandering in;
A white broom sweeping sand,
A wall falling.

Coming in, waiting for small waves,
You are bounced like a ball.
Now! Swim with the swell
And put your feet down
Waist deep. Hold out your hand
To the lifeguard who seizes it
And pulls like a tractor saying
'Coom! Coom!' as the wave
Withdraws on the steep beach
And the sand with it
So you run against a tide
Of sand and water as the next wave
Crashes behind you and hits you hard;
But thanks to the man you're high enough,
Knee deep and safe so you thank him
And thank God and laugh.

Behind you the waves surge
Like the sea breathing.

ROUND THE WORLD

A ship comes home
Gleaming with gold:
Shining on the sails
Lying in the hold.
The strange ship glows
Like a golden rose.

The men aboard
Were brown and thin
And every one
Wore a golden chain.
The sea was tame.
Another ship came

And hailed the first,
'Vat ship?' '*The Desire*,
Captain Can'dish.'
'Vere you from?' inquired
The Flemish man
As the two ships ran

Softly to the Sound.
'Ah that'd be telling.
Barbary and Borneo.'
Laughter came swelling
From the barely moving ship
That seemed to trip

The measured waves.
'Vy you have sails like dat?'
'We thought we'd gild them
No! We took a fat
Galleon in the south sea.
We're out o' sailcloth, totally.'

So we sail with the best brocade.
What news? We've had none this trip.'
'King Pheellip he sends sheeps.
Drake he send fire sheeps.
Sheeps go back, long vay.
Not many get back, dey say.'

'They're been up to mischief.
And, we've missed all the fun.'
The Desire sailed on glittering
In the declining sun:
Of the brilliance the wind was fond,
Golden fish in the silver pond.

DAILY WALK

Every day she walked down
To the sea: estuary really
But from the beach you could
Look out to open sea.
Every day she wandered down
Past primroses, then elderflower,
Sea lavender, blackberries
And frosted twigs to stare out
Over the North Sea.

It was there two years ago;
Ten years ago; twenty years ago
That her only son went down
With his torpedoed ship.
So she walked to the river
Every day; a small
Deliberate woman
Shuffling down and gazing
Far out to sea.

MARY'S ROBE

Blue world from my window;
Quarter green, olives, turf and brambles;
All the rest is purest blue; mountains
Sea and sky wash each other blue;
The colour cradles, dream blue.
Far to the left a broken farmhouse
Shows the tide is still running out.
The sea that flows like a robe
Round Italy is not enough.

Not enough vines and figs; no virtue
In the olive tree. The deserted cats
Glare from an overgrown garden.
Coathanger hawk suspends emptiness.
Down the awkward track no sound
But cowbells. The evening sea is veined
With violet. Wild boars come here
For roots. Foreign guests come
From far away for quietness.

HYMN MODERN

Oh worship the King
Who does not exist.
From each beautiful thing
Pray let us desist.
Community centred;
Antiracially right;
We feel we have entered
The realms of the bright.

Oh sing of our rights!
Oh tell of our pride!
The robe isn't light
We're here for the ride.
The Scriptures erasing,
(Oh what a relief!)
We've a powerful, bracing,
Beliefless belief.

This earth with its store
Of wonders untold
Was made by the power
Of science evolved.
By accident founded;
By Big Bang decree;
The land is surrounded
By sewage and sea.

Frail children of lust;
Great Sex is our rule.
We don't feel disgust.
Abortion is cool.
Through star signs and things new
Our fantasies range;
And gladly we rise to
The challenge of change.

Oh marvellous cars!
Ineffable skill!
The world and its bars
We wander at will.
Through all of creation
We grab from the shelves.
With true adoration
We worship ourselves.

CUP BEARER

Here Harry lived
And planted the wallnut
That's grown green wings
Over the cottage.

For fifty years
He and his wife
Whirled in harmony
On the merry-go-round
Of an up-a-down world.

He was short and stocky.
His hair stood up
And what he liked
Was helping people.

The pampered peonies
He watered; ivory,
Porphyry; are pierced
Through and through now
With dark nettles.

The hymns we sang
Rose like a tower
Held securely
By Harry's base.

The silver tulip
Communion cup.
We couldn't afford
To insure, was concealed
In Harry's cottage.

He never had
A foreign holiday,
Colour television,
Videos, a good car.

He always had
Lavender, sausages,
Bacon, daffodils,
Potatoes, lilies,
And a confiding smile.

GARDEN BY THE SEA

Waterfall to flagstones,
Wisteria, the scent flows
Carrying happiness:

Scarlet, amber, mauve azaelas blaze
Under the Maple;
Wide Oak, awake at last,
Tosses a green skirt:
Cuckoo jubilant
Over buttercups.

But the sea,
Chameleon to the sky,
Implies all this is gaudy nonsense
Which we must leave
And go out on the tide.

TREE FROM THE TAGUS

Crablike I carry a can
To the tub and tilt.
Clear wings spread out
Each side of the pillared stem,
Too frail for the canopy;
Too ordinary to pump
Water up to the green globes.
Or so it seems. The leaves
Have changed; longer and lighter
Than when they arrived; to trap
Our distant sun. Last year's oranges
Are lemon now. This year's are dark green
And about the size of plums.
Sometimes I count them,
Triumphing
In the orange generosity.
In May we moved
Through fragrant air;
Watching the bees
Lift to the white.
In October,
When the misty curtains draw
Across the day,
I must ask two strong men
To heave the tree in
To the orangery.
Every evening I worship here
With holy water and due reverence
For the miracle of trees.

PLASTIC COUNTRY

You would think there was a lake
By the road: but it's
A plastic lake, pregnant
With potatoes;
Bringing them on that vital
Fortnight earlier.

Sometimes when they put
The plastic down, Spring wind
Tears it up and clothes
The trees like Christo:
Or the wildest wash day
You ever saw.

Put on with skill and trouble.
Taken off with trouble.
We grow food in the old way
But now there are machines.
Do they make us
Different?

Less labour, more leisure, but what's
The effect of endless noise?
Machinery synchronises
With most men's power drive.
So are nearly all women
Left out again?

REMISSION

After digging three dull days,
Oh what labour to walk the dogs
In a miasmic country; blaring bullocks,
Complaining vulture crows, the rain
Tap-dancing on you and the ground:
I woke to the sun, coming like a vast ship
To alter everything for the exhausted castaways.
Going out, without a coat, I savoured
The placid dazzle; the more because
It would not last: the top of the arc
Barely lifted over the trees; the top of its strength
Barely lit the stage for eight acts.
Yet while the sun continued to sing
Everyone joined chorus; the river echoed
Splendour, the birds reminded us
They were still in the trees, the holly berries
Hit the note, the children shouted
And the people smiled, even the out of work,
Even the old felt the accursed depression
Would one day evaporate.
But the best was the first
After the long journey through your mind
Opening your eyes and every feeling
Registering 'The sun!'

SACKVILLE COUSINS

He wasn't brought up at Knole
So although he was
Rich enough to live there
He said he found it triste.

She was brought up at Knole
So although she couldn't live there —
It would never be hers — dreaming
She was always running up the painted stairs.

He was Uncle Davey
Gemütlich Germany flowed
From his fingers
As he played in the red room.
Over the soufflé the microscope
Of his talk showed you
The thing, enlarged, exact, exact.

She was Orlando.
With the flaming sword
Of the entail turning towards them
They wandered through beamy deserts,
She and her observant husband;
Till they recovered a castle
And conjured an arctic garden.

She never came again
And he came seldom.
The courts and corridors,
Lord Amherst's ivory throne.
The strange beasts on the stairs
Were without them.

CHARM

Driving along, shook up
On a bumpy track,
I looked down at a puddle
Embroidered with goldfinches.
Red shouts, gold sings
On head and wings;
Bits of glittering water
Slung about.

No doubt it was too good
To last, although I came
Slowly, quietly,
They cleared out fast.

SURVIVORS

The Essex Emerald
Has perished.
The Silky Wave
Is hanging
By a thread.
The Kentish Glory
Is only

In Aberdeenshire.
The Hook Tip
Is hung up
On small-leafed limes.

But softness may
Still flourish
And powdered wings
Go wandering
In the night.

Brussels Lace
Still weaves about.
The Barberry Carpet
Can be found
Underfoot.
The Marsh Mallow
Is soft
In Sussex.
The Moon Moth
Is shining
In the night.

TWILIGHT

Early in the evening
When owls begin to call
And her husband was leaving,
She saw a meteor fall.

The in between time. The smell
Of after-rain was strong.
She asked him as the bells
Bounced, 'Will you be long?'

No answer. She saw the patches
Of dim daffodils she'd thinned.
The practice bells threw snatches
Of sound into the wind.

'When will you be back?'
The weird white owl's clever
Wings planed to the black
Through the pink. 'Never.'

He said, 'I'm going to Jane.'
The whine, then the murmur
Of the car as the pain
Like waves swept over her.

FLIGHT

I woke to flapping; 'curtain' I thought as I lay
But when I looked there was a small bird
On the window. It was the wings I'd heard.
I rose and went across; the brilliant day
Rushed in; long tailed and slim, its head was
                                                          grey,
Its waistcoat yellow; picked up it stirred
Within my hands and called, a double word,
Released it sped and soon was far away.

All parents hold a bird within their hand.
Be gentle then, the wings are very frail.
You may have quite forgotten flying though
You soared once. You cannot understand
Their songs; and all too often you will quail
To see the risks they run but let them go.

DECOY POND

Stagnant water calls as the relentless sun
Irons blades and petals
To brown felt. The waterfall
Appears to thread a singing ribbon
Through the leaves.

The pond is wide and welcome as a bed
To the exhausted. Tearing off my clothes
I step down into amber.
Sand and cool. The sweat dries.
The worries calm. Brandy thrusts by,
A torpedo.

I speak to her; a straight tail lifting
Whisks the water. Blue nymphs and wasps
Lurk on every lily leaf. Past me,
A foot away, skims a kingfisher.
Oh stay! That blue! He's gone! How cool I am!
How happy! But still our trees parch in
July furnace.

THE FIRST

While she helped cut up
The antelope under
The fire-bright tree
She saw the small wolf
Creeping closer, wagging its tail
And licking its lips, so
She threw it a piece of liver.

'Why?' said her mother
Pulling back the tough shoe hide
While a lion roared behind the hill.
'My wolf' she said, laughing
And walked towards it. The wolf
Rolled over and she scratched
Its pink and white belly.

'Bite' warned her husband,
Coming back with a dead flamingo
Over his shoulder. 'Not bite',
She said, 'My wolf.' As she bent
The child on her back reached out
His hands and the wolf licked them.

Her father came, carrying a spear.
'Bad!' he said as she threw
Another bit of liver to the wolf.
'Not bad, Father, my wolf hunts.
Wolf stand. Out comes buck.
I throw spear. Kill buck.'
Her father shook his shaggy head.

'Not good women hunt.'
He considered. 'Wolf smell?'
'Yes! Yes!' she said laughing,
Scratching her wolf while the kites
Called overhead. 'Wolf smell.
Wolf hunt for us.
We eat well.'

THE GOLDEN RING

After a stormy passage
I came to haven;
And finding daffodils;
Cool gales

That fan the glade;
Chocolate;
Pleasure in bed;
Kissing and children:
I never
Put to sea any more.

WRONG ANIMAL

The Knight of Kerry
Is called George.
By some oversight
The Knight of Kerry's
Cook's dog
Is called George.
It clogs the wheels
For when the Dame of Kerry
Calls the Knight
She gets the dog.
And when the cook
Calls the dog
She gets the Knight.

NEW LIFE

Plum blossom
Billowing
About the peak
Of Clare's house.
When her body went crazy
She lived for a week
In just such a billowing bubble.
Leukaemia.

It was a long winter.
The doctors had to tell
The parents there was no hope;
No hope at all; but suddenly
It was spring. Driving past
And seeing the immaculate ice-cream
I was glad Clare
Could see it too.

QUACK

Yesterday I saw
A shellduck.

It was just walking along;
Wagging its head;
Doubting I was safe
As I drove by.
It was so white,
So black, so chestnut,
So patterned, it looked like
An abstract
But better.

SUDDEN DEATH

A kestrel
Is celestial;
And only a mouse
Which is terrestrial,
Could tell you why
The kestrel
Hangs on high;
Fanning, fanning,
In the sky.

APPARITION

A heron scrapes
Over the slate.
Bubbles burst from the lake.
The water twitches, slaps
And hatches otters.

They play porpoising
Rolling over, sleek
As malachite,
Sinuous as waterweed
Love play in the lake bed.

At our feet they tumble
In the sun; then the bubble bursts,
The birds have flown
And only ripples run
To the stiff lilies.

FAR FLOWERS

Mark, whose architecture
Is better than his botany,
Asked me
If the orchids,
Mauve and marvellous
Were nasturtiums.

DRISHANE

The house rang in cuckoo - clamour.
He sang all evening; a blacksmith
Beating our worries to better shape;
With the power of Spring he spelled out
That the frail hold on the old house
Would nevertheless be strong.

Light, space and elegance where once
Two girls took a fancy to write
Of the tumultuous life around them.
The Irish RM. A time machine
To restore the decorous drawing room
And the chaotic kitchen.

The double cuckoo, carolling
Somewhere in curtain trees disclosing view:
Plays orchestra to perfection;
Lawn, haven and point. The house solidly
Attends; weather-slated, fan-lighted,
Wrapped in a gentle Georgian dream.

The women of the house watch
Composed and coping; wooden frames
Now enclose them. Although the times
May have turned against them, the cuckoos
And the Somervilles are still
Flourishing here and singing.

MY FATHER

I hope he would be satisfied
If he could see the country now.
The young trees stand beside the ride:
Although we've not a single cow.

If he could see the country now
He'd know we've done just as he'd wish.
Although we've not a single cow
The chain of ponds are stocked with fish.

He'd know we've done just as he'd wish.
The irrigation's stronger now
The ponds that still are full of fish
Are dimpled by the willow boughs.

The irrigation's stronger now.
The ponds he stocked so long ago
Are dimpled by the willow boughs.
On to the land the water flows.

The ponds he stocked so long ago;
The young trees stand beside the ride;
On to the land the water flows:
I hope he would be satisfied.

HORSE POWER

He threw a spotlight
From now to then,
That dying man,
So in the little pool of light
I saw the scene glowing with longing
For the old people and the old ways.

'I was a'ploughin'
In the back end.
End of the war that were.
Fine morning I remember
After frost. Your father come
In that white van
And you with him
Runnin' out and callin'
"Mr Cole! Mr Cole!
Can I feed your horses?
I've brought them some carrots."
"Why yes," I said,
"They'll relish those."
You held your hand out flat,
Bold as brass and them old horses
Fairly towered over you.
No matter for that,
They was kind enough.'

He died next week.
The parson told me
He sent his regards.
Regards from a dead man
I met on that bright morning.

SPRING ENDING

Yet again I go
To see Richard.
He doesn't know me now.

Bees lift
To the pink japonica:
Daffodils light
The long grass:
A blackbird sings
In almond blossom
But not for him.

TOM

He walked through the long belt
Where the blue floods the wood
And fills the air with sweetness,
Dapple-dance of sun and shade,
Time caught in a leaf net.

Ninety years he had been here and five
He was away. 'You're our only hope' declared
The tense Colonel, 'He's killing so many men'.
So in his sandbagged steeple Tom watched.
Twice he had to go down to the trench below.
While the bags spun and burst but in the night
They built the lookout up again and Tom
                           watched.
Over the German lines some of the country
Was remarkably intact: trees, haystacks,
Damaged farm buildings, all of which
Had to be watched. A rifle spat
Through the gun growl and Tom heard, and saw
A slight movement in the straw, half a mile away.
Took aim and fired. Out of the haystack dived
The German sniper.

Azalea breath. The nightingales'
Probe whistle followed by
Bubble song. Cuckoo bell
And Tom was by the cottage
Where he'd lived.

'You're a fool' his mother told him, pouring tea.
'Who made me one?' He answered cheerfully,
'Not me. You don't git it from my family
I can tell you. You git home safe
You git a good job under Skelton at the Decoy
                      And what do you do next?
I'll tell you; you take up with a farmer's daugher'.
'Mother! Mother! You talk as if farmers were
                      lepers.
She is a farmer's daughter. What's wrong with
                      that?'
'Plenty! For the likes of us. Now she fancy you.
And she don't regard it, but years to come
That'll be a different story. How'll she like
Doing all her own work? She bin used to
                      servants'.
Tom's father munching home-made bread stated
'That's for her to choose an' she will and th' boy
                      here,
And you can't stop them.'

The waterfall, singing in leaves,
Is a memorial
To a powerful man. A hawk
Lives up to it's old name
'Windhover' over the wood.

He held her beside the lake while she kicked
And laughed and kicked again. Bright hair in the sun.
Gold sepals in the white petals. 'Oh!' he groaned 'Oh!
You're wetting me. Oh my word alive! I'm wholly soaked'.
His daughter screamed with triumph. 'Come you out!'
Ordered his wife from the bank. 'You're sopping wet.
Peter'll soon be back and wanting tea'. 'We're a coming.
We bin somethin' bad but now were going to be good
Aren't we?' — 'Es' said his daughter snuggled in his arms.
As they walked back they met a boy running:
'Uncle George says to tell you "Thanks for the buns and we're
Going to have a war an' we're going to lose."'
'Well you tell your Uncle George if you see him
Afore I do; we're going to have a war and we're
Going to win'.

At last he came to the lake
Clasped in wood like a full moon
Sliding out of clouds. There he found
The decoyman, putting up
Reed screens and went to help.

Down to the decoy and Mrs Baker said 'I do wish
                             you'd tell Tom
Not to go catching sparrowhawks' — 'Surely not
                             even Tom
Can catch many sparrowhawks' 'His hands were
                             scratted to pieces.
An' last winter he hardly went to bed.'
                             Turtledoves purred
As I stood by the pond and Tom, tall and grim,
Materialised. 'What's all this about
                             sparrowhawks?'
'Rum old go! That come in low after sparrows
When I was feeding duck an' before I knew I'd
                             gone
And caught it. That come of a misspent youth
                             y'know.
Too much cricketing' 'And did you never go to
                             bed last winter?'
'No! No! I got up once or twice
To break ice but I never missed a night's sleep.
Twenty was the year. I got up in January
I went to bed in March and I caught
Nine thousand fowl.'

SEA BEAST

Lap lap on the shore
In late July, sea lavender
And strawberries. A boy crouched
Where the silver licks the sand.
I asked him what he was looking at.
'A seal keeps coming.' I lolled
Beside him, sleepy in the heat,
And sure enough a round head rose
And bobbed at our feet;
Round-eyed and spell bound
The sea looked at the land.

SEA OF FAITH

'Can I come?' said Peter.
The sea clapped as he trod
The tickling waves. 'Look! Look at me!'
He yelled. 'I'm water-walking
Like a beetle. My Talmud cousins
Can't do that for all their scrolls.'

The sea charged and spat at him.
Staggering, the not unknown fear
Of deep water struck and he began
To sink. A hand clasped his,
The waves were soft steps
For his weightlessness, this was fun again,
And in his hand all the warmth in the world.

Selected Publications from New Hope International

POSITIVELY POETRY
An International Anthology of Little Press Poets, 1970-1995
Over 100 poets including Stella Browning, David Cobb, R.L.Cook, Mabel Ferrett, Eddie Flintoff, John Gonzalez, Roger Harvey, Brian Merrikin Hill, David Jaffin, Peter Thabit Jones, Anne Lewis-Smith, Nigel McLoughlin, Christopher Pilling, Andrea Sherwood, Steve Sneyd, Kenneth C Steven, John Ward, Maureen Weldon and Leo Yankevich. **Artwork** by Cato, Ian M.Emberson, John Light, Joyce Mills, Ian Robinson, Geoff Stevens and Carmen Willcox
ISBN 0 903610 16 7 -   £5.95   [£10 ex-UK]

PAUL REECE: BARBED WIRE RAINBOW.
"It's nice to see someone who can use four lines to a whole page to make his statement. Good mixture, lot of protest - but protest is valid, succinct and entertaining. Thought-provoking ....Recommended"   — *Dial 174*
ISBN 0 903610 14 0   £2   [£3 ex-UK]

B.Z.NIDITCH: ON THE EVE
"A summing up of a poetic career that scans decades and continents. The first poems are timeless stories, school days and birthdays. Further on, the enchor of history appears, with reflections on many events in Eastern Europe — Auschwitz, German culture, Stalin's death and Pasternak's. Dense with thickets of meaning, these are not poems to be casually scanned, but to be savoured and appreciated."   — *Factsheet Five.*
ISBN 0 903610 07 8   £1.50   [£2 ex-UK]

GERALD ENGLAND: EDITOR'S DILEMMA
An account of 20 years of Small Press Publishing, including original poetry by George Cairncross, Cal Clothier, Andy Darlington, John Elsberg, Peter Finch, Geoffrey Holloway, Anne Lewis-Smith, William Oxley &c.
ISBN 0 903610 10 8   £1.50   [£2 ex-UK]

ALBERT RUSSO:
PAINTING THE TOWER OF BABEL
"Truely an internationalist by background the poems selected for this pleasing and impressive collection seem to build into a wide-screen overview of the world. Russo is not tied to any one corner and lets all his experiences enter the arena. Albert Russo is an accomplished and talented user of words." — *Target.*
"At his best when trying to puzzle out the nature of reality ... features the poet's own photographs." — *Zene.*
ISBN 0 903610 18 3 £3 *[£4 ex-UK]*

BRIGGFLATTS VISITED:
A TRIBUTE TO BASIL BUNTING
Poems by Stella Browning, Gerald England, Sally Evans, Mabel Ferrett, Eleanor Makepeace, Malcolm Payne, Christopher Pilling, Colin Simms, John Ward; Articles by Chris Challis, Mabel Ferrett, Brian Merrikin Hill, William Oxley, Richard Livermore.
2nd edn. with new illustrations.
ISBN 0 903610 17 5 £3 *[£4 ex-UK]*

BRIAN BLACKWELL: THE SMILE OF LIES
In the Land of Birches, the poems which make up the second half of this collection draw on the poet's experiences in Belarus, where he was a visiting lecturer. "he deftly counterpoints the observed world with the suffering that lies just below its surface....sharp and observant" — *Target*
ISBN 0 903610 19 1 £3 *[£4 ex-UK}*

STEVE SNEYD: A MILE BEYOND THE BUS.
"Many of the titles in this book contain a reference to place. In Sneyd's poetry pre-Roman Celts and angry Luddites mingle with the industrial workers of today, and this historical but still personal perspective is one of his strongest attributes. He also shares with the old man in *Slaughter Gap* the ability to tell a compelling story" — *Crooked Roads*
ISBN 0 903610 11 6 £2 *[£3 ex-UK]*

NOVIN AFROUZ: HOPE OF PEACE
First collection by the celebrated Iranian concert pianist and winner of *The Milan Peace Prize*. "Stirred by the dawn, the sea, flowers, the Revolution, wind, the poet vibrates, is deeply moved, sings, retying in the poem the sacred bonds of music and language."
 —*Leopold Sadar Senghor* (ex-President of Senegal).
ISBN 0 903610 04 3 £1.95 [£3 ex-UK]

GLENDA WINTEIN: THE IRRESISTIBLE ROSE
"We need poets like Glenda to bring down the curtain over both over-serious modernism and owly academics in vitro of their own making and to insert between some female Falstaffery. A Grimsby girl, she is probably the first poet to get *Ovaltine* and *Woodbines* together in a ninth-decade poem, which dates her, Nevertheless poems like *Overloaded Structure* (all about the spinal column) should bring a spring to your own" — *Ore*
ISBN 0 903610 15 9 £2 [£3 ex-UK]

JOHN MARKS: LIFTING THE VEIL
"Lifting the Veil is refreshing both in the simplicity of form and in the way the poet uses words - his own and those given to others - unfussed, clear and immediate to the reader.... In all these poems the poet is visible, which also makes him vulnerable" — *Iota*
ISBN 0 903610 20 5 £3.50 [£5 ex-UK]

GERALD ENGLAND: LIMBO TIME
Pre-millennium poems, with a foreword by Mabel Ferrett. "The range is impressive: haiku, tanka, sijo, sonnets, a semi-concrete sequence of *'squares'*. Whole landscapes and ways of life can be summed up in a few lines... this is a kind of selected Gerald England, and new readers could well start here." — *Zene*
"subtle and well put together" — *Pulsar*
ISBN 0 903610 21 3 £3.75 [£5 ex-UK]

"NINETY NINETY"

A 90-min tape of poetry, music & fun featuring Chris Challis, Dave Cunliffe, Andy Darlington, Eddie Flintoff, Tom Grierson, Roger Harvey, Peter Thabit Jones, Lord Litter, Gwen Wade, John Ward, Glenda Wintein & more.   £3   *[£5 ex-UK]*

AABYE

The new and vibrant poetry magazine from New Hope International.
ISSN 1461-6033

Issue A includes collaborative poetry, translations, long poems, short poems, prose poems, haiku, englyn and lots more from an international list of authors including R.G. Gregory, Anthony Lawrence, Stephen Oliver, K.V. Skene, Steve Sneyd and Zoogirl.

Single issues are £3.75 [£5 ex-UK].
Subscriptions — 3 issues for £10 [£13 ex-UK].

NEW HOPE INTERNATIONAL REVIEW
Volume 20 #3

Original poetry by Christopher Allan, Kaye Axon, Rick Doble, David A Groulx, Gordon Hassall, Bill Headdon, Santiago Montobbio, Colin Nixon, Trish O'Brien, Michael J Reith, Nathalie Thomas, Robert Truett, Lloyd Vancil, and Gordon Wardman. **100s of reviews** of books, magazines, audio material, software, videos &c
The last printed edn.   60pp   *£3.75*   *[£5 ex-UK]*

A fuller list of titles is available for an sae or IRC.

All orders should sent to **New Hope International**, 20 Werneth Avenue, Gee Cross, Hyde, Cheshire, SK14 5NL, UK. together with payment — cheques payable to "**G. England**" (sterling only) Preferred overseas payment method is International Giro (available in sterling from Post Offices worldwide) Currency notes to the sterling equivalent will be accepted at sender's risk), or International Reply Coupons at the rate of 10 IRCS = £4. Postage and packing is extra on trade and institutional orders.